The Tiny Traveler
Joke Book
for Children!

A Tiny Traveler Book by

Clay Westfall

These jokes were all compiled by the author from jokes told to him by his children, grandchildren and other social sources. While they most likely appear in other forums, any duplication or copying is unintentional

©2013 by Clay Westfall

ISBN-13: 978-1481976138
ISBN-10: 1481976133

This book is to
David, Alex and Dmitri, three of
the funniest boys I know.

Animal Jokes

Why do bears have fur coats?
Because they would look silly in a sweater!

When is the best time to buy parakeet?
When they're going cheap!

How do cats eat spaghetti?
The same as everyone else - they put it in their mouths!

Why did the turkey cross the road?
To prove he wasn't chicken.

Why didn't the dog speak to his foot ?
Because it's not polite to talk back to your paw!

What do you give a pig with a sunburn?
Oinkment!

Where do milkshakes come from?
Cows that do aerobics!

What fish swims up the river at 100 miles per hour?
A motor pike!

What does a twelve-pound mouse say to a cat?
'Here Kitty, kitty, kitty'!

When is it bad luck to be followed by a black cat?
When you're a mouse!

Where do frogs keep their money?
In a river bank!

What animal do you look like when you take a bath?
A little bear!

Have you ever hunted bear?
No, but I've been fishing in my shorts before!

What does the lion say to his friends before they go out hunting for food?
'Let us prey.'

What do tigers wear in bed?
Stripey pajamas!

What's striped and bounces up and down?
A tiger on a pogo stick!

Where kind of coffee do birds drink?
Nest-cafe!

What do you call a cat with a shovel?
Doug!

What do you call a cat without a shovel?
Doug-less!

How do you keep a dog from barking in the back seat?
Put him in the front seat.

Dinosaur Jokes!

First Dinosaur: Did you hear about the ten tons of woolly mammoth hair that was stolen from the wig-maker today?
Second Dinosaur: No,I
haven't.
First Dinosaur: The police are now combing the area.

First Dinosaur: Ask me if I'm a rabbit.
Second Dinosaur: Okay. Are you a
rabbit?
First Dinosaur: Yes, I'm a rabbit. Now ask me if I'm a Dinosaur.
Second Dinosaur: OK, are you a
Dinosaur?
First Dinosaur: No, silly. I just told you I'm a rabbit.

First Dinosaur: What kind of bears like to go out in the rain?
Second Dinosaur: Drizzly bears.

First Dinosaur: What do you call a bee that can't make up his mind?
Second Dinosaur: A may-bee.

First Dinosaur: What do snake handlers wear around their necks?
Second Dinosaur: Boa-ties.

First Dinosaur: How do you stop a dinosaur from biting his nails?
Second Dinosaur: I give up.
First Dinosaur: Pull his foot out of his mouth.

First Dinosaur: What well-known cartoon character do moths like the best?
Second Dinosaur: Micky Moth!

First Dinosaur: What happened when the cat ate a ball of wool?
Second Dinosaur: She had a litter of mittens!

Why didn't the dinosaurs take ballet lessons?
They outgrew their leotards.

First Dinosaur: Why did the chicken cross the basketball court ?
Second Dinosaur: He heard the referee calling fowls.

First Dinosaur: What's the difference between a lemon, a dinosaur and a tube of glue?
Second Dinosaur: I give up.
First Dinosaur: You can squeeze a lemon, but you can't squeeze a dinosaur.
Second Dinosaur: What about the glue?
First Dinosaur: That's where you get stuck.

Why don't more dinosaurs join the police force?
They are too big to hide behind billboards.

Why did the dinosaur walk on two legs?
To give the ants a chance.

Why is it dangerous to go into the jungle between two and four in the afternoon?
That's when dinosaurs are jumping out of palm trees.

Why does a dinosaur climb a tree?
To get in his nest.

Why do dinosaurs have long toenails on Friday?
Because their nail person doesn't come until Saturday.

What did the man say when he saw the dinosaurs coming down the path wearing sunglasses?
Nothing! He didn't recognize them.

More Animal Jokes!

How do you catch a runaway dog ?
Hide behind a tree and make a noise like a bone!

What dog loves to take bubble baths?
A sham-poodle!

What kind of dog does a vampire prefer?
Any kind of bloodhound!

What dogs are best for sending telegrams?
Wire haired terriers!

What do you call a happy Lassie?
A jolly collie!

What do you call a nutty dog in Australia?
A dingo-ling!

What kind of dog sniffs out new flowers?
A bud hound!

What is the dogs favorite city?
New Yorkie!

Why do spiders make good baseball players?
They can catch fly's!

Why did the chicken cross the road, roll in the mud and cross the road again ?
Because he was a dirty double-crosser

How do you start a teddy bear race?
Ready, teddy, go!

Why didn't the chicken skeleton cross the road?
Because he didn't have enough guts!

Why did the chicken cross the playground?
To get to the other slide!

Why did the turtle cross the road?
To get to the shell station.

Why did the horse cross the road?
Because the chicken needed a day off.

What do you get if you cross a teddy bear with a pig?
A teddy boar!

What do you get if you cross a fish with an elephant?
Swimming trunks!

What do you get if you cross a skunk with a bear?
Whinnie the Pooh!

What do you get if you cross a kangaroo with a sheep?
A wooley jumper!

Why is polar bear cheap to have as a pet?
It lives on ice!

Why shouldn't you take a bear to the zoo?
Because he'd rather go to the movies!

What is a bear's favorite drink?
Coca-Koala!

Why is the desert wolf everyone's favorite at Christmas?
Because he has sandy claws!

What does a lion brush his mane with?
A catacomb!

What did the lion say when he was eating the clown?
This tastes funny!

How can you get a set of teeth put in for free?
Smack a lion!

What birds spend all their time on their knees?
Birds of prey!

What do you call a woodpecker with no beak?
A head banger!

Why is a sofa like a roast chicken?
Because they're both full of stuffing!

What kind of bird is always rude?
A mockingbird!

How does a hurt bird manage to land safely?
With its sparrow-chute!

What is green and pecks on trees?
Woody Wood Pickle!

What do you get if you cross a cat with a parrot?
A carrot!

Why did the chicken cross the road?
To get to the other side.

How do cats eat spaghetti?
The same as everyone else - they put it in their mouths!

What is a French cat's favorite pudding?
Chocolate mousse!

What do cat actors say on stage?
Tabby or not tabby!

What did the cat say when he lost all his money?
I'm so paw!

How do you know if your cat has eaten a duckling?
She's got that down in the mouth look!

What do you get if you cross an elephant with a Kangaroo?
Great big holes all over Australia!

What is small, cute, cuddly, and purple?
A Koala holding its breath!

What is the difference between an elephant and a flea?
An elephant can have fleas but a flea can't have elephants!

Why did the elephant paint his toenails red?
So he could hide in the cherry tree !

How do you know when there is an elephant under your bed ?
When your nose touches the ceiling!

What do you call an elephant that flies?
A jumbo jet!

What do you get if you cross an elephant and a kangaroo?
Big holes all over Australia!

What happens when a frogs car breaks down?
It gets toad away!

What kind of dog can tell the time?
A watch dog!

How does an elephant get down from a tree?
He sits on a leaf and waits till autumn!

Why did the elephant paint himself with different colors?
Because he wanted to hide in the coloring box!

Why were the elephants thrown out of the swimming pool ?
Because they wouldn't hold their trunks up!

What time is it when an elephant sits on the fence ?
Time to fix the fence!

Why does an elephant wear sneakers ?
So that he can sneak up on mice!

What do cows like to dance to?
Any kind of moosic you like!

What do you get if you cross a steer with a tadpole!
A bullfrog!

What game do cows play at parties?
Moosical chairs !

What do you get from a dizzy chicken?
Scrambled eggs !

What do you give a pony with a cold?
Cough Stirrup !

Where do milkshakes come from?
Excited cows!

Why do ducks have webbed feet?
To stamp out forest fires !

What do you get if a sheep walks under a cloud ?
A sheep that's under the weather !

Why did the rooster cross the road?
To cockadoodle dooo something.

First Pig: Why did the little girl take hay to bed?
Second Pig: To feed her nightmare.

First Pig: Why did the rabbit go to the doctor?
Second Pig: Because he felt jumpy.

**First Pig: What happened to the two bedbugs
who fell in love?**
Second Pig: They were married in the Spring.

First Pig: Why can't you tell secrets on a farm?
Second Pig: Because the corn has ears, the potatoes
have eyes, the grass whispers and the horses carry
tails.

What did the vet call the sick pony?
A little hoarse!

What do you call an elephant in a phone box?
Stuck, probably!

Why did the rabbit go to the doctor?
He felt a bit jumpy.

First Pig: What did the Cinderella fish wear to the ball?
Second Pig: Glass flippers.

First Pig: What's smarter than a talking horse?
Second Pig: A spelling bee.

First Pig: What did the duck say when it laid a square egg?
Second Pig: Ouch.

First Pig: When is it socially correct to serve milk in a saucer?
Second Pig: When you're feeding the cat.

First Pig: How do you tell the difference between an elephant and a rhinoceros?
Second Pig: The elephant has a better memory.

First Pig: What does a frog say when it washes car windows?
Second Pig: Rub it, rub it, rub it.

Gorilla: I'm feeling terrible, Doctor. I keep thinking I'm a Great Dane.
Doctor: How long have you been feeling this way?
Gorilla: Since I was a puppy!

How come the giant Ape climbed up the side of the skyscraper?
The elevator was broken!

How did a Gorilla come to be with Washington at Valley Forge?
He had seen a sign saying, 'Uncle Simian Wants You!'

How do you know that owls are smarter than chickens?
Have you ever heard of a Kentucky fried owl?

What do you get if you cross a parrot with a woodpecker?
A bird that talks in Morse code!

What happened to the owl that lost his voice?
He didn't give a hoot!

What do mice do when they're at home?
Mousework!

What kind of musical instrument do mice play?
A mouse organ.

Why do mice have long tails?
Well, they'd look silly with long hair!

Who has large antlers, a high voice and wears white gloves?
Mickey Moose.

How do you save a drowning mouse?
Use mouse to mouse resuscitation!

Where do hamsters come from?
Hamsterdam!

What's a mouse's least favorite record?
What's up Pussycat!

Why do mice need oiling?
Because they squeak!

What's the difference between an injured Lion and a wet day?
One pours with rain and the other roars with pain!

Who has eight guns and terrorizes the ocean?
Billy the Squid!

How do you keep a dog from crossing the road?
You put him in a barking lot.

Why did the pigs cross the road with their laundry?
They wanted to do their hogwash.

Did you hear about the two kangaroos who crossed the road?
They jumped into each other's pouches and were never seen again.

What do you call a fish with no eyes?
A FSH!

What do sardines call submarines?
Cans of people!

Why did the one-handed gorilla cross the road?
To get to the secondhand shop.

What do you call a chicken that crosses the road without looking both ways?
Dead.

Why did the hen go halfway across the road and stop?
She wanted to lay it on the line.

Why did the frogs cross the road?
To get a croak-a-cola.

Why did the sheep cross the road?
He needed to go to the baa-baa shop.

Why did the rabbit cross the road?
To get to the hopping mall.

Why did the wasp cross the road?
It needed to go to the waspital.

First Chicken: What kind of math do owls like?
Second Chicken: Owl-gebra.

What kind of snake is good at math?
An adder.

What do you get if you cross a parrot and a centipede?
A walkie talkie!

Why does a stork stand on one leg?
Because it would fall over if it lifted the other one!

What do you get if you cross a bumble bee with a door bell ?
A humdinger !

How do fish go into business?
By starting out on a small scale!

Where do you weigh whales?
At a whale-weigh station!

What did the bookworm say to the librarian ?
Can I burrow this book please !

Billy: My dog plays chess
Willy: Your dog plays chess, he must be clever! **Billy: Not really, I usually beat him three times out of four!**

Why are dolphins smarter than People?
Because they can train us to stand by the pool and feed them!

If twenty dogs run after one dog, what time is it?
Twenty after one!

"Who's been eating my porridge", squeaked Baby Bear. "Who's been eating my porridge", cried Mother Bear. "Burp!", said Father Bear

What do bee's chew?
Bumble gum.

Why are skunks always arguing?
Because they like to raise a stink!

How do you milk a mouse?
You can't, the bucket won't fit underneath!

What do reindeer say before telling you a joke?
This one will sleigh you!

Why do reindeer wear fur coats?
Because they would look silly wearing a blanket!

How do you make a slow reindeer fast?
Don't feed it!

Why did the reindeer wear black boots?
Because his brown ones were all muddy!

How long should a reindeer's legs be?
Just long enough to reach the ground!

Why did the reindeer wear sunglasses at the beach?
Because he didn't want to be recognized!

Which reindeer have the shortest legs?
The smallest ones!

Where do you find reindeer?
It depends on where you leave them!

What do reindeer have that no other animals have?
Baby reindeer!

What powerful reptile can be scene at the theater?

The Lizard of Oz!

How do you give a chameleon a nervous breakdown ?
Put him on a checkered rug !

What did one firefly say to the other?
I've got to glow now!

What kind of tiles can't you stick on walls ?
Reptiles !

What jumps up and down in front of a car?
Frog-lights !

What happened when a frog joined the cricket team?
He bowled long hops !

Why do bee's hum?
Because they forgot the words!

What kind of bull doesn't have horns ?
A bullfrog !

Why is it better to be a grasshopper than a cricket?
Because grasshoppers can play cricket but crickets can't play grasshopper!

What kind of bees drop things all the time?
Fumble bees!

What does a confused bee say?
To bee or not to bee!

What looks like half a cat?
Just like the other half!

What do you get if a sheep walks under a cloud?
A sheep that's under the weather!

Where do shellfish go to borrow money ?
To the prawn broker !

What do you call a big fish who makes you an offer you can't refuse ?
The Cod-father !

How could the shrimp afford to buy a house ?
He prawned everything !

Which fish can perform operations ?
A Sturgeon !

What happened to the shark who swallowed a bunch of keys ?
He got lockjaw !

What is green and can jump a mile in a minute?
A grasshopper with hiccups!

Where do fish wash?
In a river basin!

Why did the whale cross the road ?
To get to the other tide !

Where do little fishes go every morning ?
To little fish school!

What do you call a bee who has had a magic spell put on him??
Bee witched!

What goes zzub zzub?
A bee flying backwards!

What goes 99 clonk!! 99 - clonk!!
A centipede with a wooden leg!

What do you get from a bad-tempered shark ?
As far away as possible !

Do Apes kiss?
Yes, but never on the first date!

Do you know a favorite expression used by the Gorillas?
Apesy daisy!

How do you tell where a flea has bitten you?
Just start from scratch!

What did one flea say to the other flea after a night out?
Should we walk or take the dog?

What do you call a bee born in May?
Maybe's!

What is a bees favorite rock star?
Sting!

What is a bee's favorite rock group?
The BEE GEE's!

More Silly Jokes

How do you stop a head cold from going to your chest ?
Easy - tie a knot in your neck !

Why shouldn't you swim on a full stomach ?
Because it's easier to swim on a full swimming pool !

What animal lives on the bottom of sheep ships ?
Baaa-nacles !

How can you tell if your little brother is turning into a refrigerator?
See if a little light come on whenever he opens his mouth!

What has four wheels and flies?
A garbage truck!

What is black and white and red all over?
A skunk with diaper rash!

What is the coldest part of the North Pole?
An explorer's noes !

What do computer operators eat for lunch?
Chips!

Why is that man standing in the sink?
He's a tap dancer !

Where do rabbits learn to fly?
In the Hare Force!

Why did the hen cross the road?
To prove she wasn't chicken !

How do you stop a rooster crowing on Sunday morning?
Have him for dinner on Saturday night!

What do you call a man with a tree growing out of his head ?
Ed-Wood !

What do you call a woman with a sheep on her head?
Baa-Baa-Ra!

What do you call a man who wears tissue paper trousers ?
Russell !

What do you call a nun with a washing machine on her head ?
Sister Matic !

How did the telephones get married ?
In a double ring ceremony !

Why did the child study in the airplane ?
He wanted a higher education !

Why was the broom late ?
It over swept !

Do you know the time?
No, we haven't met yet!

What kind of hair do oceans have?
Wavy Hair!

What runs but never walks?
Water!

How do you make milk shake?
Give it a good scare !

What's red and flies & wobbles at the same time?
A jelly copter !

How do fleas travel?
They itch hike!

What is an insects favorite game?
Cricket!

Customer: Waiter, this soup tastes funny!
Waiter: Then why aren't you laughing?

Why did the clock get sick ?
It was run down !

Why did the man with a pony tail go to see his doctor ?
He was a little hoarse !

What do you call a witch flying through the sky?
Broom Hilda !

What do you call a chicken at the North Pole?
Lost!

What did the silly boy call his pet zebra ?
Spot !

What do you call a fish on the dining table ?
Dinner!

What do you call a man whose father was a Canon?
A son of a gun !

What do you call a man with two left feet ? Whatever you like - if he tries to catch you he'll just run round in circles !

What do you call a weekly television program about people staying clean?
A soap opera !

First penguin: "They say that swimming is a very good exercise for keeping slim.
Second penguin: "Oh yeah? Have you ever seen a whale?

What do cats read in the morning?
Mewspapers!

**There were four cats in a boat, one jumped out.
How many were left?**
None. They were all copy cats!

What is a cat's favourite color?
Purrr-ple

What do you call a bee that complains a lot?
A Grumble bee!

Billy: "Have you ever seen a man-eating fish?" ?
Silly: "Yes."
Billy: "Where?"
Silly: "Yes, in a seafood restaurant!"

When do you need a swimming suit for horseback riding?
When you are riding a sea horse!

What do you call a fish with two knees?
A two-knee-fish!

What do you get if you cross a sheep and a space ship?
Apollo neck woolly jumpers!

What do you get if you cross a box of matches and a giant?
The big match!

What do you get if you cross a kangaroo with a skyscraper?
A high jumper!

What do you get if you cross a road with a safari park?
Double yellow lions!

How do you keep a fish from smelling?
Hold its nose!

What do you call a crab that talks a lot?
A gabby crabby!

Why did the fly fly?
Because the spider spied her!

What game did the cat like to play with the mouse?
Catch!

Where did the school kittens go for their field trip?
To the mewseum.

What kind of cats like to go bowling?
Alley cats!

Why did the flea fail his exams?
He wasn't up to scratch!

What do you call a fly with no wings?
A walk!

Why wouldn't they let the butterfly into the dance?
Because it was a moth ball!

How does a flea get from place to place?
By itch-iking!

What did one flea say to the other flea?
Shall we walk or take the dog?

What's smaller than an ant's mouth?
An ant's dinner!

Where would you put an injured insect?
In an ant-bulance!

What has four wheels and flies?
A rubbish bin!

How do we know that insects are so clever?
Because they always know when your eating outside!

What do insects learn at school?
Mothmatics!

What's the biggest moth in the world?
A mammoth!

Why is it better to be a grasshopper than a cricket?
Because grasshoppers can play cricket but crickets can't play grasshopper!

What is green and can jump a mile in a minute?
A grasshopper with hiccups!

What did one firefly say to the other?
Its time for me to glow!

What's small and cuddly and bright purple?
A koala holding his breath!

What happens when a cat eats a lemon?
It becomes a sour puss!

Why are elephants wrinkled?
Have you ever tried to iron one?

What do you get if you cross a fish with an elephant?
Swimming trunks!

Why do elephants never forget?
Because nobody ever tells them anything!

What day do fish hate?
Fry-day.

Why do cats make terrible story tellers?
They only have one tail.

What do cats eat for breakfast?
Mice Crispies.

Why did the cat run away from the tree?
Because it was afraid of the bark!

What do call bears with no ears?
B!

Where do cows go on Saturday nights?
To the MOOO-vies!

Why is it hard to play cards in the jungle?
There are too many cheetahs!

When is it bad luck to see a black cat?
When you're a mouse!

What time is it when an elephant sits on your fence?
Time to get a new fence!

What does a kitten become after it's three days old?
Four days old!

What kind of animal goes OOM?
A cow walking backwards!

What is a crocodile's favorite game?
Snap

What happens when a frog's car breaks down?
He gets toad away.

What do you get when you cross a parrot with a pig?
A bird who hogs the conversation.

What do you call a rabbit with a sun tan?
A sunny bunny!

What do you get if you cross a crocodile with a flower?
I don't know, but I'm not going to smell it!

Why is it so hard for a leopard to hide?
Because he's always spotted.

What happened when the dog went to the flea circus?
He stole the show!

What's the difference between an injured lion and a wet day?
One pours with rain, the other roars with pain!

What animal has more lives than the cat?
A frog, he croaks every night.

What is the strongest animal?
A snail. He carries his house on his back!

What is the difference between a flea and a wolf ?
One prowls on the hairy and the other howls on the prairie!

What did the clean dog say to the insect ?
Long time no flea!

How do you find where a flea has bitten you?
Start from scratch!

What do you call an elephant in a phone box?
Stuck!

What do you get when you cross a porcupine with a balloon?
A great big POP!

Where do hamsters come from?
Hamsterdam.

What kind of snake is good at math?
An adder.

Why are igloos round?
So polar bears can't hide in the corners!

Why was the dog so sweaty?
He was a hotdog!

What kind of dog likes baths?
A Shampoodle!

What dog keeps the best time?
A watch dog!

What do you get if you cross a cocker spaniel, a poodle and a rooster?
Cockerpoodledoo

What do you give an elephant with big feet?
Plenty of room!

What's gray and squirts jam at you?
A mouse eating a doughnut!

Why aren't elephants allowed on beaches?
They can't keep their trunks up!

What has six eyes but cannot see?
Three blind mice!

Jimmy: I lost my dog.
Cindy: Why don't you put an ad in the newspaper?
Jimmy: Don't be silly! He can't read

How does a hedgehog play leap-frog?
Very carefully!

What do you call a gorilla wearing ear-muffs?
Anything you like! He can't hear you!

What do you give an elephant that's going to be sick?
Plenty of space!

Why do swallows fly south in winter?
It's too far to walk!

What bird is always out of breath?
A puffin!

How do you keep a rooster from crowing on Sunday morning?
Have him for dinner on Saturday night!

What do you call a chicken at the North Pole?
Lost!

What did the little bird say to the big bird?
Peck on someone your own size!

Which bird does construction work?
The crane!

Why do dogs run in circles?
Because it's hard to run in squares!

When do vampires like horse racing?
When it's neck and neck.

What kind of weather excites a pet duck?
Fowl weather, of course!

What do you call a boring bird at the beach?
A dull gull!

Did you hear the story about the peacock?
It's a beautiful tail!

What bird is with you at every meal?
A swallow!

What do you call a rooster that crows every morning?
An alarm cluck!

What do you call a sick eagle?
Ill-eagle!

What do you get if you cross cereal with a canary?
Shredded TWeet!

When is a duck ten feet tall?
When he is on stilts!

Why do cowboys ride horses?
Because they're too heavy to carry!

What did the horse say when it fell?
"I've fallen and I can't giddyup!"

What's worse than a giraffe with a sore throat?
A centipede with sore feet!

What steps do you take when a bear is chasing you?
Very big ones!

More Dinosaur Jokes!

What do you do when a dinosaur sneezes?
Get out of the way!

What do you call a dinosaur wearing tight shoes?
My-foot-is-saurus!

What do you get when two dinosaurs collide?
Tyrannosaurus wrecks!

Why are there old dinosaur bones in the museum?
Because they can't afford new ones!

What do you do when a dinosaur sneezes?
Get out of the way!

What do you call a dinosaur wearing tight shoes?
My-foot-is-saurus!

What do you get when two dinosaurs collide?
Tyrannosaurus wrecks!

Why are there old dinosaur bones in the museum?
Because they can't afford new ones!

Receptionist: Doctor, there's an invisible dinosaur in the waiting room.
Doctor: Tell her I can't see her!

Why did the dinosaur cross the road?
Because the chicken was on vacation.

What makes more noise that a dinosaur?
Two dinosaurs!

What does a Triceratops sit on?
Its Tricera-bottom!

What is the difference between a horse and a duck?
One goes quick and the other goes quack!

What's a horse's favorite sport?
Stable tennis.

What do you give a sick horse?
Cough stirrup.

What do you call a blind dinosaur?
I-don't-think-he-saw-us!

What was T Rex's favorite number?
Eight (ate)!

What do you get when two dinosaurs collide?
Tyrannosaurus wrecks!

What did the dinosaur say after the car crash?
I'msosaurus!

What do you call a tyrannosaurus that talks and talks and talks?
A dinobore!

What do you call a Stegosaurus with carrots in its ears?
Anything you want, it can't hear you!

What do you call a dinosaur that never gives up?
Try-Try-Try-ceratops!

First Dinosaur: "Look at all these fly's! Do you think we should shoo them"?
Second Dinosaur: "No, just let them fly barefooted".

When can three giant dinosaurs hide under a small umbrella and not get wet?
When it's not raining!

First Dinosaur: "How many apples do you think we can get from that tree"?
Second Dinosaur: "None".
First Dinosaur: "Why"?
Second Dinosaur: "It's a pear tree".

What's the best way to talk to a dinosaur?
Long distance!

Which type of dinosaur could jump higher than a house?
Any kind! A house can't jump!

Why don't dinosaurs ever forget?
Because nobody ever tells them anything!

What does a giant Tyrannosaurus eat?
Anything she wants!

What should you do if you find a dinosaur in your bed?
Find somewhere else to sleep!

Did the dinosaur take a bath?
Why, is there one missing?

Patient: Doctor, doctor, I keep seeing dinosaurs with orange spots!
Doctor: Hmmm.....have you seen an eye doctor?
Patient: No, just dinosaurs with orange spots.

What do you get when a dinosaur walks through the strawberry patch?
Strawberry jam!

Fairy Tale Jokes

Why couldn't Cinderella use horses to pull the Pumpkin Coach?
Because they were too busy playing stable tennis!

Why was Cinderella no good at playing hockey?
Because she was always running away from the ball!

What do you say when the three bears want to sit down?
Three chairs for the Three Bears!

Where do mermaids go for a movie?
The Dive in!

What's green and runs through the forest?
Moldylocks!

Where did the three little pigs go for lunch?
To a pig-nic!

Why did Goldilocks have trouble sleeping?
She kept having night-bears!

Whey does the big bad wolf look like a sweet cute bunny rabbit?
When he wears a sweet cute bunny rabbit suit!

What's brown, furry and has twelve paws?
The Three Bears!

What's the difference between Mommy Bear's porridge, Daddy Bear's porridge and Baby Bear's porridge?
Well, one is Mommy Bear's, one is Daddy Bear's, and one is Baby Bear's!

When Goldilocks spilled the milk, how did she mop it up?
She used a sponge-cake!

Why did Goldilocks fall asleep?
She was listening to the three bores!

Which is the coldest fairy-tale?
Goldilocks and the Three Berrrrs!

**Why did Goldilocks stir the porridge
so fast?**
Because Daddy Bear came in and told her to beat it!

**Why wasn't Mummy Bear's porridge warm
enough?**
Because it was left over from yesterday!

Why weren't the porridge bowls round?
Because porridge is a square meal!

**What did the woodcutter's wife say to her
husband in December?**
Not many chopping days left until Christmas!

Do giants eat Englishmen with their fingers?
No, they eat their fingers separately!

**How did Jack know how many beans his cow
was worth?**
He used a cow-culator!

Jack stole a golden harp from the giant. Why couldn't he play it?
Because it took a lot of pluck!

What did Little Red Riding-Hood say when she saw the big, bad wolf wearing sun-glasses?
Nothing . . . she didn't recognize him!

What did Little Red Riding-Hood say when she saw the big, bad wolf?
There's the big, bad wolf!

Who shouted "stinky!" at the big, bad wolf?
Little Rude Riding Hood!

Jack was always a grubby boy. You know what they say?
You can lead a boy to water but you can't make him wash!

What kind of pet did Aladdin have?
A flying car-pet!

What did Aladdin do when he lost his lamp?
He used a candle instead!

On which side of the house did Jack grow the beans?
On the outside!

The giant could smell an Englishman a mile away, so he knew that there was an intruder in the castle. The gates were locked, so how had Jack got inside?
Intruder window!

What did the beanstalk say to Jack?
Stop picking on me!

What do you call a contented giant?
One that's fed up with Englishmen!

What do you get if you cross Jack's chicken with a road-builder?
I don't know, but wherever it works the streets are laid with gold!

What goes: MUF OF EIF IF?
A giant walking backwards!

What is higher than a giant?
A giant's hat!

What would you call a golden egg in a frying-pan?
An unidentified frying object!

Where was the first magic bean found?
On a magic beanstalk!

Where was the first beanstalk found?
Growing in the ground!

Why did Jack's cow have horns?
Because its bell

Why did the chicken lay golden eggs?
Because if she dropped them they would dent the floor!

Knock knock Jokes

Knock, knock.
Who's there?
Fee.
Fee who?
**Fee fie fo fum I smell the blood
of an Englishman!**

Knock, knock.
Who's there?
Sarah.
Sarah who?
Sarah giant living here?

Knock, knock.
Who's there?
Nobel.
Nobel who?
No bell so I knocked.

Knock, knock.
Who's there?
Ashe
Ashe who?
God bless you!

Knock, knock.
Who's there?
Boo.
Boo Who?
Well you don't have to cry about it!

Knock, knock.
Who's there?
Egbert.
Egbert who?
Egg but no chicken!

Knock, knock.
Who's there?
Godfrey.
Godfrey who?
Godfrey tickets to the Giant's Ball.
Want to come?

Knock, knock.
Who's there?
Paul.
Paul who?
Paul the rope and raise the drawbridge please!

Knock, knock.
Who's there?
Hugh.
Hugh who?
Yoo-hoo yourself!

Knock Knock
Who's there?
Jess!
Jess who?
I give up, who?

Knock Knock
Who's there?
Jess!
Jess who?
Jess one of those things!

Knock, knock
Who's There?
Dewey
Dewey who?
Dewey have to do our homework tonight?

Knock knock
Who's there?
Ivor!
Ivor who?
Ivor good mind not to tell you now!

Knock knock
Who's there?
Ivory!
Ivory who?
Ivory strong like Tarzan!

Knock, knock
Who's there?
Yukon.
Yukon who?
Yukon say that again!

Still more jokes!

What's brown and hairy and can see just as well from either end?
A bear with its eyes shut!

What does a shark eat on his sandwich?
Peanut butter and jelly fish!

What is the strongest animal in the ocean?
A mussel!

Which is the oldest tree in the forest?
The elder!

What kind of tie does a pig wear?
A Pig sty!

How does a pig go to the hospital?
In a Hambulance!

What do you call a pig with three eyes?
A piiig!

Why didn't the pig listen to his father?
Because he was a boar!

The End

(We hope you enjoyed it!)

Printed in Great Britain
by Amazon